| | DATE DUE | | |
|---|---|---|---|
| | | | |
| | | | |
| | | | |
| | | | |
| | | | |
| | | | |
| | | | |
| | | | |
| | | | |
| | | | |
| | | | |

# The Supreme Court

KNOW YOUR GOVERNMENT

# The Supreme Court

Leon Friedman

CHELSEA HOUSE PUBLISHERS
NEW YORK   NEW HAVEN   PHILADELPHIA

KG1-012086

3  5  7  9  8  6  4  2

**Library of Congress Cataloging-in-Publication Data**

Friedman, Leon.
  The Supreme Court.
  (Know your government)
  Bibliography: p. 89
  Includes index.
  1. United States. Supreme Court—Popular works.
I. Title. II. Series: Know your government (New York, N.Y.)
KF8742.Z9F73  1987  347.73'26  86-20798

ISBN 0-87754-825-0  347.30735


General Editor: Professor Fred L. Israel
Project Editor: Nancy Priff
Art Director: Maureen McCafferty
Series Designer: Anita Noble
Chief Copy Editor: Melissa R. Padovani
Project Coordinator: Kathleen P. Luczak

**ABOUT THE COVER**

The Supreme Court emblem, which is an adaptation of the Great Seal of the United States, is distinguished by a solitary star below the American eagle. The star symbolizes the judicial power granted by the Constitution to "one Supreme Court." Clockwise from top, photographs illustrate the Supreme Court under Chief Justice William Howard Taft (seated at center), a frieze of justice from the Supreme Court building, and integration in the classroom—the subject of several major Supreme Court decisions.

# CONTENTS

# KNOW YOUR GOVERNMENT

Other titles in this series include:

The American Red Cross
The Bureau of Indian Affairs
The Center for Disease Control
The Central Intelligence Agency
The Children, Youth, and
    Families Division
The Department of Agriculture
The Department of the Air Force
The Department of the Army
The Department of Commerce
The Department of Defense
The Department of Education
The Department of Energy
The Department of Health
    and Human Services
The Department of Housing
    and Urban Development
The Department of the Interior
The Department of Justice
The Department of Labor
The Department of the Navy
The Department of State
The Department of
    Transportation
The Department of the Treasury
The Drug Enforcement Agency
The Environmental
    Protection Agency
The Equal Opportunities
    Commission
The Federal Aviation
    Administration
The Federal Bureau of
    Investigation
The Federal Communications
    Commission
The Federal Elections
    Commission

The Federal Railroad
    Administration
The Food and Drug
    Administration
The Food and Nutrition Division
The House of Representatives
The Immigration and
    Naturalization Service
The Internal Revenue Service
The Interstate Commerce
    Commission
The National Foundation on the
    Arts and Humanities
The National Park Service
The National Science Foundation
The Presidency
The Securities and
    Exchange Commission
The Selective Service System
The Senate
The Small Business
    Administration
The Smithsonian
The Supreme Court
The Tennessee Valley Authority
The U.S. Information Agency
The U.S. Arms Control and
    Disarmament Agency
The U.S. Coast Guard
The U.S. Commission on
    Civil Rights
The U.S. Fish and Wildlife Service
The U.S. Mint
The U.S. Nuclear Regulatory
    Commission
The U.S. Postal Service
The U.S. Secret Service
The Veteran's Administration

# INTRODUCTION

# Government: Crises of Confidence

## Arthur M. Schlesinger, jr.

From the start, Americans have regarded their government with a mixture of reliance and mistrust. The men who founded the republic did not doubt the indispensability of government. "If men were angels," observed the 51st Federalist Paper, "no government would be necessary." But men are not angels. Since human beings are subject to wicked as well as to noble impulses, government was deemed essential to assure freedom and order.

At the same time, the American revolutionaries knew that government could also become a source of injury and oppression. The men who gathered in Philadelphia in 1787 to write the Constitution therefore had two purposes in mind. They wanted to establish a strong central authority and to limit that central authority's capacity to abuse its power.

To prevent the abuse of power, the founding fathers wrote two basic principles into the new Constitution. The principle of federalism divided power between the state governments and the central authority. The principle of the separation of powers subdivided the central authority itself into three branches—the executive, the legislative, and the judiciary—so that "each may be a check on the other." The *Know Your Government* series focuses on the major executive departments and agencies in these branches of the federal government.

The Constitution did not plan the executive branch in any detail. After vesting the executive power in the president, it assumed the existence of "executive departments" without specifying what these departments should be. Congress began defining their functions in 1789 by creating the Departments of State, Treasury, and War. The secretaries in charge of these departments made up President Washington's first cabinet. Congress also provided for a legal officer, and President Washington soon invited the attorney general, as he was called, to attend cabinet meetings. As need required, Congress created more executive departments.

Setting up the cabinet was only the first step in organizing the American state. With almost no guidance from the Constitution, President Washington, seconded by Alexander Hamilton, his brilliant secretary of the treasury, equipped the infant republic with a working administrative structure. The Federalists believed in both executive energy and executive accountability and set high standards for public appointments. The Jeffersonian opposition had less faith in strong government and preferred local government to the central authority. But when Jefferson himself became president in 1801, although he set out to change the direction of policy, he found no reason to alter the framework the Federalists had erected.

By 1801 there were about 3,000 federal civilian employees in a nation of a little more than 5 million people. Growth in territory and population steadily enlarged national responsibilities. Thirty years later, when Jackson was president, there were more than 11,000 government workers in a nation of 13 million.

The federal establishment was increasing at a faster rate than the population.

Jackson's presidency brought significant changes in the federal service. He believed that the executive branch contained too many officials who saw their jobs as "species of property" and as "a means of promoting individual interest." Against the idea of a permanent service based on life tenure, Jackson argued for the periodic redistribution of federal offices, contending that this was the democratic way and that official duties could be made "so plain and simple that men of intelligence may readily qualify themselves for their performance." He called this policy rotation-in-office. His opponents called it the spoils system.

In fact, partisan legend exaggerated the extent of Jackson's removals. More than 80 percent of federal officeholders retained their jobs. Jackson discharged no larger a proportion of government workers than Jefferson had done a generation earlier. But the rise in these years of mass political parties gave federal patronage new importance as a means of building the party and of rewarding activists. Jackson's successors were less restrained in the distribution of spoils. As the federal establishment grew—to nearly 40,000 by 1861—the politicization of the public service excited increasing concern.

After the Civil War the spoils system became a major political issue. High-minded men condemned it as the root of all political evil. The spoilsmen, said the British commentator James Bryce, "have distorted and depraved the mechanism of politics." Patronage, by giving jobs to unqualified, incompetent, and dishonest persons, lowered the standards of public service and nourished corrupt political machines. Office-seekers pursued presidents and cabinet secretaries without mercy. "Patronage," said Ulysses S. Grant after his presidency, "is the bane of the presidential office." "Every time I appoint someone to office," said another political leader, "I make a hundred enemies and one ingrate." George William Curtis, the president of the National Civil Service Reform League, summed up the indictment. He said,

> The theory which perverts public trusts into party spoils, making public employment dependent upon personal favor and not on proved merit, necessarily ruins the self-respect of public employees, destroys the function of party in a republic, prostitutes elections into a desperate strife for personal profit, and degrades the national character by lowering the moral tone and standard of the country.

The object of civil service reform was to promote efficiency and honesty in the public service and to bring about the ethical regeneration of public life. Over bitter opposition from politicians, the reformers in 1883 passed the Pendleton Act, establishing a bipartisan Civil Service Commission, competitive examinations, and appointment on merit. The Pendleton Act also gave the president authority to extend by executive order the number of "classified" jobs—that is, jobs subject to the merit system. The act applied initially only to about 14,000 of the more than 100,000 federal positions. But by the end of the 19th century 40 percent of federal jobs had moved into the classified category.

Civil service reform was in part a response to the growing complexity of American life. As society grew more organized and problems more technical, official duties were no longer so plain and simple that any person of intelligence could perform them. In public service, as in other areas, the all-round man was yielding ground to the expert, the amateur to the professional. The excesses of the spoils system thus provoked the counter-ideal of scientific public administration, separate from politics and, as far as possible, insulated against it.

The cult of the expert, however, had its own excesses. The idea that administration could be divorced from policy was an illusion. And in the realm of policy, the expert, however much segregated from partisan politics, can never attain perfect objectivity. He remains the prisoner of his own set of values. It is these values rather than technical expertise that determine fundamental judgments of public policy. To turn over such judgments to experts, moreover, would be to abandon democracy itself; for in a democracy final decisions must be made by the people and their elected representatives. "The business of the expert," the British political scientist Harold Laski rightly said, "is to be on tap and not on top."

Politics, however, were deeply ingrained in American folkways. This meant intermittent tension between the presidential government, elected every four years by the people, and the permanent government, which saw presidents come and go while it went on forever. Sometimes the permanent government knew better than its political masters; sometimes it opposed or sabotaged valuable new initiatives. In the end a strong president with effective cabinet secretaries could make the permanent government responsive to presidential purpose, but it was often an exasperating struggle.

The struggle within the executive branch was less important, however, than the growing impatience with bureaucracy in society as a whole. The 20th century saw a considerable expansion of the federal establishment. The Great Depression and the New Deal led the national government to take on a variety of new responsibilities. The New Deal extended the federal regulatory apparatus. By 1940, in a nation of 130 million people, the number of federal workers for the first time passed the 1 million mark. The Second World War brought federal civilian employment to 3.8 million in 1945. With peace, the federal establishment declined to around 2 million by 1950. Then growth resumed, reaching 2.8 million by the 1980s.

The New Deal years saw rising criticism of "big government" and "bureaucracy." Businessmen resented federal regu-

11

lation. Conservatives worried about the impact of paternalistic government on individual self-reliance, on community responsibility, and on economic and personal freedom. The nation in effect renewed the old debate between Hamilton and Jefferson in the early republic, although with an ironic exchange of positions. For the Hamiltonian constituency, the "rich and well-born," once the advocate of affirmative government, now condemned government intervention, while the Jeffersonian constituency, the plain people, once the advocate of a weak central government and of states' rights, now favored government intervention.

In the 1980s, with the presidency of Ronald Reagan, the debate has burst out with unusual intensity. According to conservatives, government intervention abridges liberty, stifles enterprise, and is inefficient, wasteful, and arbitrary. It disturbs the harmony of the self-adjusting market and creates worse troubles than it solves. Get government off our backs, according to the popular cliché, and our problems will solve themselves. When government is necessary, let it be at the local level, close to the people. Above all, stop the inexorable growth of the federal government.

In fact, for all the talk about the "swollen" and "bloated" bureaucracy, the federal establishment has not been growing as inexorably as many Americans seem to believe. In 1949, it consisted of 2.1 million people. Thirty years later, while the country had grown by 70 million, the federal force had grown only by 750,000. Federal workers were a smaller percentage of the population in 1985 than they were in 1955—or in 1940. The federal establishment, in short, has not kept pace with population growth. Moreover, national defense and the postal service account for 60 percent of federal employment.

Why then the widespread idea about the remorseless growth of government? It is partly because in the 1960s the national government assumed new and intrusive functions:

12

affirmative action in civil rights, environmental protection, safety and health in the workplace, community organization, legal aid to the poor. Although this enlargement of the federal regulatory role was accompanied by marked growth in the size of government on all levels, the expansion has taken place primarily in state and local government. Whereas the federal force increased by only 27 percent in the 30 years after 1950, the state and local government force increased by an astonishing 212 percent.

Despite the statistics, the conviction flourishes in some minds that the national government is a steadily growing behemoth swallowing up the liberties of the people. The foes of Washington prefer local government, feeling it is closer to the people and therefore allegedly more responsive to popular needs. Obviously there is a great deal to be said for settling local questions locally. But local government is characteristically the government of the locally powerful. Historically, the way the locally powerless have won their human and constitutional rights has often been through appeal to the national government. The national government has vindicated racial justice against local bigotry, defended the Bill of Rights against local vigilantism, and protected natural resources against local greed. It has civilized industry and secured the rights of labor organizations. Had the states' rights creed prevailed, there would perhaps still be slavery in the United States.

The national authority, far from diminishing the individual, has given most Americans more personal dignity and liberty than ever before. The individual freedoms destroyed by the increase in national authority have been in the main the freedom to deny black Americans their rights as citizens; the freedom to put small children to work in mills and immigrants in sweatshops; the freedom to pay starvation wages, require barbarous working hours, and permit squalid working conditions; the freedom to deceive in the sale of goods and securities; the freedom to pollute the environment—all freedoms that, one supposes, a civilized nation can readily do without.

"Statements are made," said President John F. Kennedy in 1963, "labelling the Federal Government an outsider, an intruder, an adversary. . . . The United States Government is not a stranger or not an enemy. It is the people of fifty states joining in a national effort. . . . Only a great national effort by a great people working together can explore the mysteries of space, harvest the products at the bottom of the ocean, and mobilize the human, natural, and material resources of our lands."

So an old debate continues. However, Americans are of two minds. When pollsters ask large, spacious questions—Do you think government has become too involved in your lives? Do you think government should stop regulating business?—a sizable majority opposes big government. But when asked specific questions about the practical work of government—Do you favor social security? unemployment compensation? Medicare? health and safety standards in factories? environmental protection? government guarantee of jobs for everyone seeking employment? price and wage controls when inflation threatens?—a sizable majority approves of intervention.

In general, Americans do not want less government. What they want is more efficient government. They want government to do a better job. For a time in the 1970s, with Vietnam and Watergate, Americans lost confidence in the national government. In 1964, more than three-quarters of those polled had thought the national government could be trusted to do right most of the time. By 1980 only one-quarter was prepared to offer such trust. But by 1984 trust in the federal government to manage national affairs had climbed back to 45 percent.

Bureaucracy is a term of abuse. But it is impossible to run any large organization, whether public or private, without a bureaucracy's division of labor and hierarchy of authority. And we live in a world of large organizations. Without bureaucracy modern society would collapse. The problem is not to abolish bureaucracy, but to make it flexible, efficient, and capable of innovation.

Two hundred years after the drafting of the Constitution, Americans still regard government with a mixture of reliance and mistrust—a good combination. Mistrust is the best way to keep government reliable. Informed criticism is the means of correcting governmental inefficiency, incompetence, and arbitrariness; that is, of best enabling government to play its essential role. For without government, we cannot attain the goals of the founding fathers. Without an understanding of government, we cannot have the informed criticism that makes government do the job right. It is the duty of every American citizen to *Know Your Government*—which is what this series is all about.

*After the Constitution established the Supreme Court, President Washington appointed the first Court justices.*

# ONE

# A Unique Institution

The United States Supreme Court is an extraordinary governmental institution. Like other courts, it settles disputes and administers justice in legal matters. But its remarkably broad, far-reaching powers set it apart from other courts.

Because of its wide range of powers, the Supreme Court's actions affect Americans in many ways. For example, the nation's schools are now racially integrated because the Supreme Court declared school segregation by race unconstitutional. Similarly, Supreme Court decisions declared that public schools can't require students to salute the flag or pray, and that school boards can't remove books from libraries because they don't like the ideas presented in them. Supreme Court rulings also help ensure that no person is sent to prison until he has exercised certain rights guaranteed to him by the government, such as the right to a lawyer and the right to have witnesses at his trial. Still other Supreme Court decisions require the states to divide legislative districts so they're represented equally.

When people think of a court, they usually imagine an institution that settles individual disputes; for example, in civil law, when one person charges another with negligent driving or when one company accuses another of breaking a contract. In criminal law, a court may decide whether a person violated the law and must go to jail. But the Supreme Court rules on cases that go beyond individual disputes and simple criminal trials. In fact, no other court has ever had the power to make such a wide range of decisions. Because the Supreme Court's decisions affect the lives of Americans in so many ways, they are more like the pronouncements of an elected legislative body, such as Congress, rather than those of a typical court.

Where does the Supreme Court get the power to make such decisions? From its unique responsibility for interpreting the Constitution, the document that founded—and still guides—the United States government.

After the American Revolution, the nation's founding fathers met in Philadelphia to frame the Constitution. Among other things, they planned to outline the powers of the federal court system—and especially the Supreme Court—in the Con-

*Supreme Court rulings ensure that a defendant can have witnesses at his trial.*

stitution. The state court systems already had supreme courts that acted as courts of appeal for the lower state courts. The founding fathers wanted to construct a similar court system at the national level. With that in mind, they included this clause in Article 3 of the Constitution: "The judicial power of the United States shall be vested in one Supreme Court, and in such inferior courts as the Congress may from time to time ordain and establish."

No one knew exactly what the responsibilities of the Supreme Court and the federal courts would be. The framers of the Constitution knew that the Supreme Court would interpret federal laws (laws passed by Congress) as well as treaties ratified by the Senate. They also expected the Court to interpret the Constitution in some way. These powers are also stated in Article 3 of the Constitution: "The judicial power shall extend to all cases . . . arising under this Constitution, the laws of the United States, and treaties. . . ."

But the founding fathers thought that, initially, the state courts would interpret the federal Constitution, laws, and treaties, and the Supreme Court would make sure that every state interpreted federal law the same way. Some thought the court system needed this final appeal to ensure uniform judgments among all state courts.

The men who framed the Constitution thought that the nation's court system might need lower federal courts for special cases, such as admiralty cases (suits involving shipwrecks, accidents at sea, or loss of goods carried on ships). They knew that the state courts wouldn't be able to handle these cases because such incidents happened outside state borders. They also believed that lower federal courts might be needed in case a citizen of one state were to sue a citizen of another state. In this type of case, called a diversity case, either state court might be prejudiced in favor of its citizen. The lower federal courts could also hear criminal cases that involved federal laws.

*Federal courts must rule on cases involving shipwrecks.*

Then, as foreseen by the founding fathers, the Supreme Court would take appeals from these lower federal court cases as well as the state court cases that involved the federal Constitution, laws, and treaties. In addition, the Supreme Court would hear cases involving foreign ambassadors and suits involving disputes between two state governments.

According to the founding fathers, the Supreme Court would have a limited role. It would take appeals from state courts on issues of Constitutional and federal law to ensure their uniform interpretation. It would also take appeals from lower federal courts on admiralty, diversity, and federal criminal cases. In cases involving ambassadors and the states, it would have original jurisdiction (power to hear a case directly instead of through an appeal).

To some people, the Supreme Court's functions didn't seem important. In fact, they seemed so insignificant that one of

President George Washington's nominees to the Supreme Court, Robert Harrison, turned down the offer. Instead, he took the post of chancellor of Maryland, a state court position. Similarly, one of the first Supreme Court justices, John Rutledge, resigned after two years to become chief justice of the South Carolina Court of Common Pleas. (He later regretted his decision and asked President Washington to reappoint him as chief justice of the Supreme Court. Washington nominated him, but the Senate refused to confirm him.)

In 1787, the Supreme Court's original role might not have been impressive. However, it was destined to change dramatically in the next thirty years.

*Rutledge left the Supreme Court for a state court position.*

*The signing of the Constitution in 1789, as shown in this painting, established the Supreme Court.*

# TWO

# Early Influences on the Court

In the nation's early years, three events occurred that transformed the Supreme Court from a limited court to a major governmental institution: the ratification of the Bill of Rights (the Constitution's first ten amendments) in 1791, the Supreme Court decision in the *Marbury v. Madison* case in 1803, and its decision in the *Martin v. Hunter's Lessee* case in 1816.

## The Bill of Rights

The Constitution was drafted in 1787. However, it couldn't take effect until it was ratified, or approved, by nine states. Antifederalists, people who didn't like the new Constitution, opposed its ratification. Federalists, those who supported the Constitution, worked to ratify it. Three of the Constitution's framers— James Madison, Alexander Hamilton, and John Jay—wrote *The Federalist Papers*, which supported ratification.

Why did the Antifederalists oppose the Constitution? Mainly because it didn't have a bill of rights, as the state constitutions did. At that time, the Antifederalists and others wanted a written constitution to protect their freedoms and to define which powers belonged to the federal government. They also wanted a bill of rights to specifically prohibit governmental infringement of individual rights to freedom of religion and speech. And as they reflected on the importance of England's Magna Charta, which limited the king's absolute power, and Bill of Rights, which guaranteed certain individual freedoms, they realized that they wanted a similar document to offer these

*The Bill of Rights guarantees individual freedoms.*

*Madison felt the courts should guard individual rights.*

protections to Americans. During the revolutionary war, each colony replaced its charter with a new state constitution that included its own bill of rights. Each state's bill of rights guaranteed freedom of religion, freedom of the press, and freedom from unreasonable search. They also guaranteed the right to trial by jury in any criminal case. Antifederalists were seeking a federal bill of rights similar to the states' versions to protect the same freedoms.

The founding fathers recognized this oversight and promised to correct it by passing a federal bill of rights as soon as the new government was formed. Many states ratified the federal Constitution on the condition that Congress pass a bill of rights as soon as possible. After the Constitution was ratified in 1789, the new federal government was organized and the founding fathers immediately acted on their promise. In June of 1789, James Madison introduced the Bill of Rights into Congress. In a famous speech, he told the Congress why the Bill of Rights was necessary and desirable, emphasizing the court system's role in protecting individuals' freedoms.

*Black power advocate exercises freedom of speech— a freedom granted by the Bill of Rights.*

Madison's speech suggested that the courts would have a special responsibility to interpret the Bill of Rights and protect the freedom and rights of the people against infringements from the executive (president) and legislative (Congress) branches of government. He said that if the Bill of Rights were incorporated into the Constitution, "independent tribunals of justice will consider themselves ... the guardians of those rights; they will be an impenetrable bulwark against every assumption of power in the legislative or executive; they will be naturally led to resist every encroachment upon rights expressly stipulated for in the Constitution by the declaration of rights." His statements implied that the courts would have the power to stop the executive and the legislative branches of the government from taking actions that violated the Bill of Rights. This power would give the federal courts, and particularly the Supreme Court, a unique position in the government. Shortly after Madison's speech, Congress passed the Bill of Rights, and in 1791, the states ratified it.

Madison did not explain how the courts would guard the people's rights against infringement by governmental branches. He didn't say that the courts would be allowed to declare laws unconstitutional or to limit the president's actions. But he certainly intended that the courts would have the power to issue orders to protect the people's guaranteed rights when the proper cases came before them.

Above all, Madison and others wanted to ensure freedom against tyranny. To help keep the federal and state governments in balance, they provided for the separation of power among the executive, legislative, and judicial branches, making it unlikely that one branch of the government would dominate the others and threaten the people's liberty. Although the founding fathers believed in a representative form of government— one in which the people would vote for representatives who would then pass laws to govern them—they also expressed concern about "the tyranny of the majority." If the majority were to vote for laws that oppressed a minority—by denying a particular group the right to vote, to practice its religion, or to hold property, for example—then some institution should have the authority to stop them. According to Madison, that institution would be the court system empowered to enforce the Bill of Rights.

The federal courts, and ultimately the Supreme Court, would have a special role as protector of the people's rights for another reason. The Bill of Rights contained rather vague and general clauses, such as "due process of law," "freedom of speech," and "unreasonable searches and seizures." Some institution had to have the final word in interpreting the Bill of

Rights in individual cases. In *The Federalist Papers*, Hamilton wrote, "The interpretation of the laws is the proper and peculiar province of the courts." And just as he foresaw, the interpretation of the Constitution became the "proper and peculiar province" of the United States Supreme Court.

Of course, the Supreme Court did not become a powerful institution overnight. Many years passed before it began to act as the special guardian of the rights described in the Bill of Rights.

## The *Marbury* Case

The second important event that changed the Supreme Court's role was the *Marbury v. Madison* case, which it decided early in 1803. Just before leaving office in March 1801, President John Adams had appointed William Marbury justice of the peace for

*Hamilton said the Court should interpret the Constitution.*

*In the* Marbury *case, Marshall added to the Court's power.*

the District of Columbia. However, when President Thomas Jefferson took office, James Madison, the new secretary of state, refused to recognize Marbury's appointment. Marbury filed a lawsuit with the Supreme Court asking for a special court order, called a mandamus, to require Madison to recognize Marbury's position.

At the time, John Marshall was the chief justice of the Supreme Court, the fourth in its eleven years. Historians consider Marshall to be one of the greatest justices and acknowledge him as the architect of the Supreme Court's special role in our government. His first chance to increase the Supreme Court's power and prestige came in the *Marbury* case.

Only two weeks after hearing the *Marbury* case, Marshall wrote the Supreme Court's opinion. The Court decided that Marbury had been improperly denied his commission (a formal

29

government document that proves a person's appointment to office). However, the Court couldn't issue a mandamus ordering Madison to recognize Marbury's commission because Marbury had brought his case directly to the Supreme Court based on the Judiciary Act, instead of starting in the lower courts and then appealing to the Supreme Court, as directed by the Constitution. (The Judiciary Act, passed by Congress in 1789, gave the Supreme Court the power to issue a mandamus in such a case under its original jurisdiction.) However, as Marshall pointed out, the Constitution had never given the Supreme Court original jurisdiction in this type of case.

Marshall declared the Judiciary Act unconstitutional, so the Court couldn't issue the mandamus that Marbury was seeking. Marshall's decision established the following three propositions that became the basis for the Supreme Court's special role in our government:

First, he said that if a law passed by Congress conflicts with the Constitution, the law is invalid. In other words, the Constitution is supreme in our government and any legislation contrary to it is invalid.

Second, he said the courts are responsible for interpreting the law and the Constitution. He echoed Hamilton's words in *The Federalist Papers* when he said, "It is emphatically the province and duty of the judicial department to say what the law is." Thus, Madison's prediction about the Bill of Rights had come true; the courts had a special role in interpreting the Bill of Rights and the entire Constitution in any case that came before it. In addition, its decision was final and had to be followed by all other branches of government.

Third, the Supreme Court could declare an act of Congress unconstitutional as part of its responsibility to interpret the Constitution and to define its terms authoritatively.

The effects of this decision might not appear to have much impact at first glance, but on closer examination, the effects are far-reaching. For instance, even if the people *unanimously* elected representatives to Congress and they *all* voted for a law that the president signed, Marshall's decision implies that a simple majority of the Supreme Court could declare that law unconstitutional. This could occur because the Constitution is supreme over any law, and because the courts—particularly the Supreme Court—are responsible for interpreting the law.

At first, not everyone accepted these propositions. President Thomas Jefferson objected to the idea that the courts are ultimately responsible for interpreting the Constitution. He questioned the notion that judges alone should be the "ultimate arbiters of all constitutional questions" and called it a "very dangerous doctrine indeed." President Andrew Jackson agreed. After a dispute with the Court, he stated that it is the duty of the other branches of government "to decide upon the constitutionality of any bill or resolution."

*Jefferson disliked the Court's role as final interpreter of the Constitution.*

*Jackson believed other governmental branches should interpret the Constitution.*

Eventually, Marshall's view prevailed. Years later, the Supreme Court wrote that "the federal judiciary is supreme in the exposition of the law of the Constitution." Of course, members of Congress and the president must interpret the Constitution almost daily in carrying out their duties. However, the Supreme Court's interpretation is "supreme" because it speaks last. Congress may pass a law that it believes is constitutional, but if someone files a lawsuit challenging that law, the Supreme Court must make the *final* decision about the law's constitutionality. Likewise, the president may take an action that he believes is constitutional, but the Supreme Court can declare that action unconstitutional if someone challenges it in court.

But the Supreme Court's power is not unchecked. Although the Court has the power to interpret the Constitution, the Constitution can always be amended. Four times in our history, the country has disapproved of Supreme Court decisions and has overruled them by passing the Eleventh, Fourteenth, Sixteenth, and Twenty-sixth Amendments to the Constitution. It is difficult to amend the Constitution: an amendment requires a two-thirds vote in Congress and a majority vote in three-quarters of the state legislatures. Therefore, the legislative branch can overrule a Supreme Court decision only if an overwhelming political majority exists. But even with this limitation, the

Supreme Court's power to interpret the Constitution and to declare acts of Congress unconstitutional has given it an extremely important role in our government.

# The *Martin* Case

In the nation's early years, the third event that helped establish the Supreme Court's role was its decision in the *Martin v. Hunter's Lessee* case. Just as the *Marbury* case defined the Supreme Court's relationship to other branches of the federal government, the *Martin* case defined its relationship to the state governments.

In the *Martin* case, two people claimed ownership of the same large piece of land. Hunter claimed ownership under state law: he bought the land from Virginia after the state had confiscated it from English sympathizers during the revolutionary war. Martin claimed ownership under federal law: he inherited

*Congress can check the Court by voting for an amendment.*

the land from his uncle, the original British owner, whose land rights were recognized by two federal treaties. The *Martin* case required the Supreme Court to determine which laws took precedence—the Virginia confiscation laws or the federal laws.

In 1813, the Supreme Court decided the case in favor of Martin and the federal treaties. However, the Virginia courts refused to abide by the Supreme Court's decision. The Virginia Supreme Court insisted that its interpretation was entitled to the same consideration as the United States Supreme Court's interpretation. It believed that the Constitution did not "restrain or annul the sovereignty of the states" and that the United States Supreme Court could not overrule its interpretation of the Constitution.

So the case went back to the United States Supreme Court in 1816. In an opinion written by Justice Joseph Story, the

*Justice Story upheld uniform interpretation of federal law in the* Martin *case.*

Supreme Court stated that its appellate power extends "to cases pending in the state courts." This means that when a federal law applies to a case in the state courts, then the case can be appealed to the United States Supreme Court. It also means that the Supreme Court's interpretation of federal law must take precedence over a state court's interpretation, and that the Supreme Court can reverse a state court decision. If the Supreme Court speaks last (after the state court has decided the question), then its interpretation is the final and authoritative one.

The decision in the *Martin* case wouldn't have surprised the framers of the Constitution. They believed the Supreme Court should review state court cases dealing with federal law to ensure uniform judgments. They included a supremacy clause in the Constitution that declared federal law should outweigh state law. This clause would be meaningless without the Supreme Court to ensure that federal law would be interpreted uniformly throughout the country.

The *Martin* case was especially important in light of the agitation for states' rights that took place before the Civil War. It demonstrated that federal law outweighed state law, and that the United States Supreme Court must have the power to review—and, if necessary, reverse—state court decisions in order for federal law to be effective.

In later years, one of the nation's greatest Supreme Court justices, Oliver Wendell Holmes, Jr., said that the *Martin* case was far more important to the United States than the *Marbury* case. He meant that the nation could have functioned as a union if the *Marbury* case had not given the Supreme Court the power to declare acts of Congress unconstitutional. But the nation could not have survived if the state courts were free to interpret federal law in their own way without the Supreme Court to ensure consistent interpretation. Fortunately, the *Martin* case established the Supreme Court's power in that respect.

# FRANK LESLIE'S ILLUSTRATED NEWSPAPER

Entered according to Act of Congress, in the year 1857, by Frank Leslie, in the Clerk's Office of the District Court for the Southern District of New York. (Copyrighted June 27, 1857.)

No. 82.—VOL. IV.]     NEW YORK, SATURDAY, JUNE 27, 1857.     [PRICE 6 CENTS.

**TO TOURISTS AND TRAVELLERS.**

We shall be happy to tender personal narratives, of local scenes, including adventures and incidents, from every person who please to correspond with our paper.

We take this opportunity of returning our thanks to our numerous artistic correspondents throughout the country, for the many sketches we are constantly receiving from them of the news of the day. We trust they will spare no pains to furnish us with drawings of events as they may occur. We would also remind them that it is necessary to make all sketches, if possible, by the earliest conveyances.

**VISIT TO DRED SCOTT—HIS FAMILY—INCIDENTS OF HIS LIFE—DECISION OF THE SUPREME COURT.**

While standing in the Fair grounds at St. Louis, and engaged in conversation with a prominent citizen of that enterprising city, he suddenly asked us if we would not like to be introduced to Dred Scott. Upon expressing a desire to be thus honored, the gentleman called to an old negro who was standing near by, and our wish was gratified. Dred made a rude obeisance to our recognition, and seemed to enjoy the notice we expended upon him. We found him on examination to be a pure-blooded African, perhaps fifty years of age, with a shrewd, intelligent, good-natured face, of rather light frame, being not more than five feet six inches high. After some general remarks we expressed a wish to get his portrait (we had made) ...

ELIZA AND LIZZIE, CHILDREN OF DRED SCOTT.

... efforts before, through correspondents, and failed), and asked him if he would not go to Fitzgibbon's gallery and ...

... have it taken. The gentleman present explained to Dred that it was proper he should have his likeness in the "great illustrated paper of the country," overruled his many objections, which seemed to grow out of a superstitious feeling, and he promised to be at the gallery the next day. This appointment Dred did not keep. Determined not to be foiled, we sought an interview with Mr. Crane, Dred's lawyer, who promptly gave us a letter of introduction, explaining to Dred that it was to his advantage to have his picture taken to be engraved for our paper, and also directions where we could find his domicile. We found the place with difficulty, the streets in Dred's neighborhood being more clearly defined in the plan of the city than on the mother earth; we finally reached a wooden house, however, protected by a balcony that answered the description. Approaching the door, we saw a smart, tidy-looking negress, perhaps thirty years of age, who, with two female assistants, was busy ironing. To our question, "Is this where Dred Scott lives?" we received, rather hesitatingly, the answer, "Yes." Upon our asking if he was home, she said,

"What white man arter dat nigger for?—why don't white man 'tend to his own business, and let dat nigger 'lone? Some of dese days dey'll steal dat nigger—dat am a fact."

DRED SCOTT, PHOTOGRAPHED BY FITZGIBBON, OF ST. LOUIS.     HIS WIFE, HARRIET, PHOTOGRAPHED BY FITZGIBBON, OF ST. LOUIS.

Newspapers focused national attention on slavery. This one featured Dred Scott (lower left) and the Supreme Court's controversial decision about slavery in his case.

# THREE

# Testing the Limits of Power

The Constitution played a unique role in the Supreme Court's development: It allocated and regulated power within the federal government, divided power between the federal and state governments, and restricted the power of the federal and state governments regarding basic rights. But the Constitution's vague phrases, such as the right to "regulate Commerce . . . among the . . . states" or the ban on "impairing the obligation of contracts," needed interpretation by some institution to ensure that their exact meaning was understood. The Constitution's effect on state government's operation was unclear. The division among the branches of the federal government wasn't clear. The state and federal governments were still testing the powers granted them by the Constitution, but no one was sure how involved the federal government should be in areas traditionally handled by the states.

Most governmental conflicts involving the Constitution eventually became lawsuits that found their way to the Supreme

Court. By the early 1800s, the people and the state governments were seeking out the Supreme Court as the best institution to settle their disputes, adding to its prestige and importance. In the years before the Civil War, the country came to view the Supreme Court as the ultimate arbiter of the great constitutional issues that confronted it and of conflicts among other governmental institutions.

In 1819, the *McCulloch v. Maryland* case clearly defined the extent of state and federal governmental power. In this case, the Supreme Court had to decide whether a state could tax bank notes—an important form of money backed by the United States Treasury and issued by the Bank of the United States. This case raised two important questions: Did Congress actually have the power to create a national bank? And did the states hold the power to impose a tax on that bank's operation? The Supreme Court's vote was unanimous. Chief Justice Marshall prepared its opinion, which said that "the power to tax is the power to destroy," and that the states could not tax or attempt to impair the federal government's important functions, such as controlling the money supply.

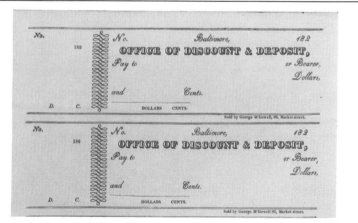

**Maryland taxed national bank notes such as these, an act that led to the *McCulloch v. Maryland* case.**

*State-restricted steamship use on the Hudson River sparked conflict over federally controlled interstate commerce.*

In the *Gibbons v. Ogden* case, the Supreme Court had to decide whether a state-granted monopoly permitting the use of steamships on the Hudson River took precedence over a federal license permitting the use of steamships in interstate commerce. The federal license permitted navigation on the Hudson despite the state's exclusive grant. The Supreme Court's decision, written by Chief Justice Marshall, stated that Congress' power under the Constitution's Commerce Clause was supreme over the states: "This power, like all others vested in Congress, is complete in itself, may be exercised to its utmost extent, and acknowledges no limitations, other than are prescribed in the Constitution." The *Gibbons v. Ogden* decision was one of the first steps in defining the extent of the federal government's commerce power and its limits on state power. It affirmed federal control over—and prevented state restriction of—foreign and interstate commerce, which stimulated the development of ports, railroads, and national commerce.

The *Charles River Bridge v. Warren Bridge* case gave the Supreme Court a chance to define further the powers of the state governments. It required the Court to interpret the part of

*A dispute over the Charles River Bridge gave the Court a chance to define state powers further.*

the Constitution that says "No state shall . . . pass any . . . law impairing the obligation of contracts." Massachusetts had originally hired the Charles River Bridge Company to build a bridge. Later, it hired a different company to build a second bridge. The Charles River Bridge Company brought a case before the Supreme Court claiming that its contract implicitly gave it a monopoly on bridge-building over the Charles River and that the state's contract with the Warren Bridge Company "impaired the obligation" of their agreement. The Court took several years to decide this case. Finally, in 1837, it ruled against the Charles River Bridge Company. In an opinion by Chief Justice Roger B. Taney, who had replaced John Marshall in 1836, the Supreme Court held that the new bridge could be built. It based this decision on the fact that the state had not *explicitly* granted a monopoly to the Charles River Bridge Company and therefore had not impaired the obligation of its contract with the company.

Another case, *Cooley v. Board of Wardens of the Port of Philadelphia*, dealt with state power. In this case, a local law required ships using the port of Philadelphia to hire local pilots or to pay a fine equal to half of the pilot's fee. One shipmaster, Aaron B.

Cooley, refused to hire a Philadelphia pilot or to pay the fine because he believed that the local law was unconstitutional. He felt that the federal government alone had the power to regulate commerce. The Supreme Court, however, upheld the local law. It said that the law dealing with pilots in the port of Philadelphia was valid and didn't conflict with Congress' power to regulate commerce. The Court's decision described two types of commerce: local commerce, which the state and local governments could regulate, and national commerce, which the state and local governments could not regulate, because it needed uniform federal rules.

The Supreme Court took on more and more of this type of conflict. They ranged from disputes between federal and state governments over the division of power to disputes between two parties claiming rights under state law when one party relied on the Constitution to support its case. These cases were

*Chief Justice Taney's statue memorializes his decisions involving state power.*

significant because they indicated how other governmental institutions were beginning to depend on the Supreme Court to resolve their conflicts.

However, the Supreme Court sometimes took on more than it could handle. Before the Civil War, the major political issue confronting the nation was slavery. The chief matter of dispute was whether Congress could forbid slavery in new states and territories. Some people thought the Supreme Court, as final arbiter of governmental disputes, should settle the issue. A case was brought before the court to decide whether a slave named Dred Scott became free when his owner took him to Illinois—a free state where slavery could not exist in any form—and then into other territories affected by the Missouri Compromise, which divided the country into a balanced number of slave states and free states.

In 1857, the Supreme Court decided the *Dred Scott* case. In a six to three vote, the justices ruled that a slave remained a slave as long as the original owner wished, because the slave was the owner's property. This decision meant that Congress couldn't pass any laws restricting slave owners' rights and that slaves had no rights at all. It also meant that free states would have to allow slavery because people could bring their slaves— their property—to these areas. And because of this, the Missouri Compromise, which established some free states, was unconstitutional.

**The Supreme Court interprets laws for local and national commerce in ports such as Philadelphia.**

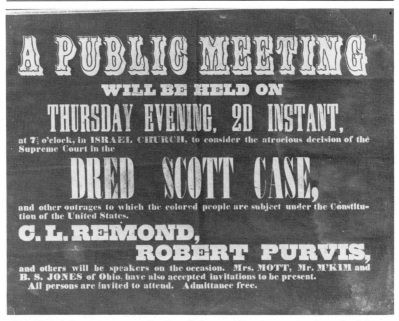

*The* Dred Scott *case polarized the nation; war was inevitable.*

Further, the decision in the *Dred Scott* case meant that slavery could exist unchecked—Congress could not admit any new free states into the union or try to restrict the spread of slavery. The Supreme Court, the final arbiter, had not supported the control of slavery. In fact, its decision made it impossible to settle the slavery conflict peacefully. If a compromise had been possible between the free states of the North and West and the slave states of the South, the Civil War could have been avoided. However, the Supreme Court had taken a firm stand against compromise and war became inevitable.

Today everyone agrees that the decision in the *Dred Scott* case was a terrible mistake. Yet the case was important because all governmental institutions expected the Supreme Court to settle the matter peacefully. This expectation showed that, by 1857, the entire country assumed that the Court was the authority on important constitutional issues.

*Child labor was common after the Civil War because Court decisions protected businesses from governmental control.*

# FOUR

# Regulating Business

During the Civil War years, the Supreme Court reached a low point in public esteem, primarily because of the *Dred Scott* decision and the fact that four of the Supreme Court justices came from the South.

After the Civil War, the Supreme Court's power began to grow again. In 1868, the states ratified the Fourteenth Amendment, which contained broad restrictions prohibiting them from depriving anyone of the "equal protection of the laws" or of "life, liberty or property without due process of law." These words were meant to protect the newly freed slaves from repressive laws passed by the southern states. But did these phrases apply to other laws as well?

Soon after the Civil War, many people urged the Supreme Court to apply the Fourteenth Amendment to other state laws. They claimed that if a state law restricted a person's ability to work at a certain job, then it deprived him of "liberty" without "due process of law." They thought if the state tried to set rail-

45

road rates, grain elevator charges, maximum work hours, or minimum wages, then the state was depriving a person or a company of "liberty or property without due process of law." No one knew if these assumptions were true, but everyone knew that it was the Supreme Court's job to confirm or deny them. For the Supreme Court was now established as the ultimate interpreter of the Constitution as well as the new amendments. People expected the Supreme Court to give these laws concrete meaning.

For a time, the Supreme Court strictly interpreted state laws that restricted business. For example, in 1890 it decided that a state could not set railroad rates if the railroad company wouldn't earn a fair profit. The reason: fixed rates would deprive the railroad of its "property." In 1897, the Supreme Court struck down Louisiana laws regulating insurance, because they restricted the citizens' "liberty" to make contracts with out-of-state insurance firms. In 1905, the Court decided that a state could not pass a law setting maximum hours for workers, because such a law would restrict the "liberty" of the worker and his company to agree on a desirable wage.

In all of these cases, the Supreme Court invalidated certain state laws that were designed to protect people from the activities of large companies that had gained economic power after the war. It did this through its power to interpret the Constitution's new amendments—a power that was now firmly established.

At the same time that the Supreme Court was restricting the states' powers, it was restricting Congress' power to regulate business. In 1895, it held that the federal income tax was unconstitutional. (This led to the passage of the Sixteenth Amendment, which granted Congress the right to pass an income tax law.) It also ruled that the Sherman Antitrust Act, a federal law designed to curb monopolies, did not apply to a busi-

*In 1890, the Supreme Court struck down state laws that tried to regulate railroad rates.*

ness controlling 98 percent of the nation's sugar manufacturing. In the same year, the Supreme Court decided that a federal court could issue an order to stop railroad workers from striking. Some years later, the Court ruled that Congress could not prohibit companies from sending products made by child labor across state lines because it had no power to regulate labor at the local level.

All of these decisions aided growing corporations by protecting them from state and federal governments that tried to control their activities. The decisions also protected the corpo-

*Political cartoons lampooned businesses that used child labor. The Supreme Court upheld the rights of businesses.*

rations from unions that tried to get higher wages and better working conditions, because strikes were viewed as activities that restricted business.

For the next 50 years, the Supreme Court decided similar cases: the state and federal governments continued to pass laws regulating business, and the corporations continued to argue that these laws violated their constitutional rights and were beyond Congress' power to enact. But many individuals believed that the Supreme Court should have been as concerned with their rights as it was with the rights of corporations.

The conflict between individuals and corporations persisted. Finally it came to a head in the 1930s. During the Great Depression, millions of people were unemployed. Farmers couldn't make enough money to survive because food prices were so low. To solve these problems, the federal government passed New Deal laws proposed by President Franklin D. Roosevelt that were designed to promote economic recovery and social reform. Many states passed similar laws to try to reduce the hardships of workers and farmers. However, the Supreme Court found many of these laws unconstitutional, either because they restricted the corporations' liberty and property or because Congress had exceeded its power.

In 1936, President Roosevelt attacked the Supreme Court's actions in declaring so many of these laws unconstitutional. He said the Supreme Court decisions created a national crisis because they made it impossible for the government to do anything about the country's major economic problems. To make matters worse, no justices had resigned or retired during Roosevelt's first term in office, so he couldn't appoint any new justices who might favor his New Deal legislation. To try to

*As soup kitchens became more common, many felt the government should make laws to promote economic recovery.*

*Above: Roosevelt announced his New Deal legislation. Right: When the Court opposed it, he developed a court-packing plan, which cartoonists quickly satirized.*

rectify the situation, Roosevelt asked Congress to approve a judicial reform proposal, which quickly became known as his "court-packing plan." In essence, the plan would have allowed Roosevelt to add an extra justice for every justice over age 70 who didn't retire. Congress considered—but didn't pass—this controversial proposal. Instead, it passed the Supreme Court Retirement Act, which made retirement more attractive to the justices.

After President Roosevelt was overwhelmingly reelected in 1936, the Supreme Court began to change its approach. In a series of decisions, the Court held that Congress could pass laws regulating business, just as John Marshall had decided in the *Gibbons* case more than 100 years before. The Court also decided that the states had wide powers to act without violating any company's "liberty or property." The Supreme Court changed its view on these laws and let the government take steps to solve the country's economic problems.

*Separate water fountains marked COLORED and WHITE exemplified the Court's "separate but equal" doctrine.*

# FIVE

# Guarding Individual Freedoms

The protection of individual freedoms has always been part of the Supreme Court's job. Even before the Supreme Court gave the federal and state governments more leeway in passing economic laws, it began to review laws that restricted the personal rights of citizens. As far back as 1791, Madison had said that the Court should be the guardian of the rights specified in the Bill of Rights. Even in its early days, the Supreme Court's decisions guarded the freedom of the people against the government. For instance, after the Civil War ended, the Court decided that the government could not require former members of the Confederacy to take special oaths before becoming lawyers or priests.

As the nation entered the 20th century, guarding the people's rights against the government became the Supreme Court's most important role. During World War I, the Court began reviewing laws that would limit freedom of speech and freedom of the press, such as the Espionage and Sedition Acts.

In 1919, it decided in the *Schenck v. United States* case that a man could be punished for giving a speech during wartime that told men to avoid military service. Justice Oliver Wendell Holmes, Jr., prepared an opinion for the Court stating that some things that could be expressed publicly in peacetime could not be expressed in wartime. He wrote that if a person said or wrote something that would produce a "clear and present danger" to the country, then he could be imprisoned. For that reason, criticism of a war that discouraged people from joining the army could be punished and would not be protected by the First Amendment, which guarantees freedom of speech and freedom of the press.

The issue came up again during the war in the case of *Abrams v. United States*. Abrams, a Russian immigrant, wrote and distributed pamphlets attacking American policy toward the new Soviet regime in Russia. In one of the pamphlets, he warned American workers not to make guns and bullets to use against the Russians. The Supreme Court held that the government could jail Abrams and four of his associates because their pamphlets could jeopardize America's defense. But Justice Holmes disagreed, contending that the defendants' actions did not necessarily constitute a clear and present danger. He believed that the lawyers had not actually proved the defendants' intent to hinder the war effort and wrote a famous opinion that supported free speech. He wrote that "the best test of truth is the power of the thought to get itself accepted in the competition of the market, and that truth is the only ground upon which their [the people's] wishes safely can be carried out." In other words, all people—including Abrams—have the right to free speech. They can say what they want—as long as their words present no clear and present danger. Listeners will discuss their words freely and decide if they are true.

In 1925, Justice Holmes wrote another dissenting opinion in the *Gitlow v. New York* case. The Court decided that a man

*Holmes wrote the Court's decision in the* Schenck *case.*

named Benjamin Gitlow had to go to jail for writing a pamphlet praising Communism. Holmes said that the Court was punishing Gitlow just for expressing his ideas, even though his ideas had not incited anyone to do anything wrong. In Holmes' opinion, "Every idea is an incitement," but expression of an idea is no reason for imprisonment.

Although Justice Holmes' view did not prevail at the time, his dissenting opinions supporting free speech and free press had a strong influence on lawyers, judges, and many other people. Gradually, the other Supreme Court justices began to rethink their views. In 1968, 50 years after Holmes first began to write on this problem, the Supreme Court accepted his view. In the *Brandenburg v. Ohio* case, the Court ruled that the only speech that could be punished was speech that incited—or was likely to incite—"imminent lawless action." This case set an important precedent: federal and state laws that tried to punish

# GITLOW LOSES FIGHT IN HIGHEST COURT TO ANNUL ANARCHY LAW

New York Left Wing Socialist's
Conviction Sustained by
7 to 2 Decision.

## STATE STATUTE IS UPHELD

Justices Holmes and Brandeis
Dissent From Doctrine Laid
Down by Colleagues. ·

## WILL APPEAL TO GOVERNOR

Civil Liberties Union Announces
Smith Will Be Asked to Pardon Him.

New York Times *headlines announced the Court's ruling in the* Gitlow *case.*

people for speaking freely would be unconstitutional unless they met the "Brandenburg test."

The Supreme Court handed down many decisions protecting the right of the press to print news and matters of public concern. In 1971, in two famous cases, the Supreme Court decided that the federal government could not prohibit *The New York Times* and *The Washington Post* newspapers from printing stories based on secret documents concerning the Vietnam War. The documents, known as the Pentagon Papers, didn't reveal any classified military plans; rather, they recounted the history of the war and how the United States became involved in it. The Court ruled that the government didn't have an adequate reason to restrain the press. In another case, the Supreme Court ruled that before a public official could sue a newspaper for libel, he would have to show that the newspaper had a "reckless disregard" for the truth in printing the story. These decisions encouraged the press to write about matters of public concern without fear of lawsuits.

The Supreme Court has overturned many laws that restricted the exercise of free speech or free press. From 1950 to 1985, it declared many federal and state laws unconstitutional because they infringed on these First Amendment rights.

The Supreme Court has also issued many opinions dealing with religious freedom. In 1943, it heard a case involving the Jehovah's Witnesses. Members of that religion believed that they should not be required to salute the American flag even in wartime because it was against their religious beliefs to do so. However, the state governments required children of Jehovah's Witnesses to salute the flag. If they refused, they would be expelled from school and their parents could be sent to jail. In the *West Virginia Board of Education v. Barnette* case, the Supreme Court decided that the state could not deprive the Jehovah's Witnesses of the free exercise of their religion by requiring them to salute the flag. The Court wrote, "If there is any fixed star in our constitutional constellation, it is that no official . . . can prescribe what shall be orthodox [required] in politics, nationalism, religion or other matters of opinion. . . ."

Years later, in a similar case, the Supreme Court held that Amish children could attend Amish schools instead of being required to attend public schools. This decision was also necessary to permit the Amish their "free exercise of religion," a right guaranteed by the First Amendment.

The Supreme Court decided that the state could not aid religions by giving money or other help to churches or schools

57

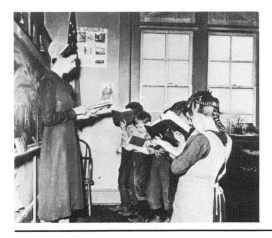

*Court rulings allow children to attend religious schools, as do the Mennonites in this classroom.*

run by religious orders. This would be "an establishment of religion" by the state, which is prohibited by the First Amendment. The same principle prohibits forced prayer in public schools. However, a city can set aside space for a Christmas nativity scene without that action being considered "establishment" of religion.

All of these decisions resulted from the Supreme Court's interpretation of the First Amendment and the Court's role as guardian of the people's rights. The Supreme Court acted as guardian of other rights as well. The Constitution's Fourth Amendment guarantees the people's right to secure their homes and possessions "against unreasonable searches and seizures." It also requires probable cause and a warrant before a police officer can search a home. To enforce this rule, the Supreme Court, in 1914, decided in the *Weeks v. United States* case that any material seized without a warrant could not be used as evidence in a criminal trial. This decision removed any incentive for the police to violate the Fourth Amendment. In 1961, the Court held in the *Mapp v. Ohio* case that this decision applied to state criminal cases as well as to federal cases. However, in 1984, the Court ruled that if a search warrant was issued by mistake, the evidence could be used in the trial.

The Supreme Court also enforced the Fifth Amendment, which states that no one can force a person to incriminate himself. In 1966, the Supreme Court decided in the *Miranda* case that a person should be warned of his constitutional rights, such as the right to a lawyer, immediately after he's arrested. The Supreme Court established the "Miranda warnings" as part of its effort to enforce the Fifth Amendment. As a result, the police must warn all suspects before questioning that they have a right to remain silent, that any statement they make may be used against them, and that they have a right to see a lawyer before or during questioning. Further, the police must tell each suspect that if he can't afford an attorney, one will be provided. If the police obtain a confession without informing a suspect of these rights, the Court will not accept it as evidence.

---

SUPERIOR COURT OF THE DISTRICT OF COLUMBIA

SEARCH WARRANT

TO: _____
(Specific Law Enforcement Officer or Classification of Officer of the Metropolitan Police Department or other Authorized Agency)

Affidavit, herewith attached, having been made before me by _____
_____that he has probable cause to believe
that on the (person) (premises) (vehicle) (object) known as _____
_____
_____
in the District of Columbia, there is now being concealed certain property, namely _____
_____
_____

which is _____ and as I am satisfied
(alleged grounds for seizure)

that there is probable cause to believe that the property so described is being concealed on the above designated (person) (premises) (vehicle) (object) and that the foregoing grounds for issuance of the warrant exists.

YOU ARE HEREBY AUTHORIZED within 10 days of the date of issuance of this warrant to search (without giving notice of identity and purpose) in the daytime/at any time of the day or night, the designated (person) (premises) (vehicle) (object) for the property specified, and if the property specified, and if the property be found there

YOU ARE COMMANDED TO SEIZE IT, TO WRITE AND SUBSCRIBE IN AN inventory of the property seized, to leave a copy of this warrant and return, to file a further copy of this warrant and return with the Court on the next Court day after its execution.

Issued this _____ day of _____ , 19____

_____
Judge, Superior Court of the District of Columbia

---

*The Court requires search warrants to help protect "against unreasonable searches and seizures."*

The Sixth Amendment guarantees every criminal defendant the right to a lawyer. This means not only that the government must allow a lawyer to represent the defendant in court, but that the state must make sure that every defendant has a competent lawyer. In 1932, after the trial of the Scottsboro boys (13 young black men accused of raping 2 white women), the Supreme Court held that a state could not appoint a lawyer on the day of the trial and expect him to represent his clients without preparation. Such an action would cheat the defendants of their rights. In later cases, such as the *Gideon* case, the Court decided that if a person could not afford a lawyer, the state would have to appoint one for him.

In two other areas, the Supreme Court has been particularly vigilant in protecting the rights of the people against governmental interference. The first area concerns the people's right to privacy. Although the right to privacy wasn't described specifically in the Constitution, it has been interpreted by the Supreme Court as a right guaranteed by the Fifth and Fourteenth Amendments (that guarantee liberty) and the Fourth

**The National Guard escorted the Scottsboro boys to court.**

*Pro-choice rally urged Court to repeal antiabortion laws.*

Amendment (that protects against unreasonable searches). This right to privacy protects people from government interference in certain important personal choices, such as whether or not to terminate a pregnancy. In 1973, the Supreme Court decided in *Roe v. Wade* that a state can't bring criminal charges against a woman who has an abortion in her first or second trimester of pregnancy. (In the third trimester, a state may limit abortions to those that must be performed to save the mother's life.) The court based this decision on its analysis of the term "liberty" in the Fourteenth Amendment. The Court said that liberty meant the right to make certain personal, private decisions about one's body and one's life without state interference.

The second area of vigilance concerns the people's right to "equal protection of the laws" guaranteed by the Fourteenth Amendment. After the Civil War, many southern states passed laws to keep blacks in an inferior position. These laws denied them the right to vote, to serve on juries, and to own land. The

Supreme Court decided that the laws denying blacks their citizenship rights violated the equal protection clause.

But what of laws that required black and white citizens to go to separate schools or to sit in separate restaurants or railroad cars—laws that simply separated the races? Did they violate the equal protection clause? At first, the Supreme Court ruled that a state could allow racial separation as long as the separate facilities were equal. This ruling became known as the "separate but equal" doctrine. However, it soon became obvious that black people would not really have equal opportunities to go to school or to earn a living. As time passed, many blacks challenged the laws requiring them to attend separate schools and limiting or prohibiting their use of buses, trains, restaurants, and so on.

Finally, in 1954, the Supreme Court made one of its most historical decisions in the *Brown v. Board of Education of Topeka* case. In its decision, the Court said that any law requiring racial

*Pro-life demonstrators disagreed with the Court's decision.*

*Activists marched in Washington to support civil rights.*

separation or segregation in schools was unconstitutional because it violated the equal protection clause of the Fourteenth Amendment.

In later years, the Supreme Court declared unconstitutional many laws that permitted racial discrimination in voting and other matters. The Court took the lead in abolishing state laws that restricted and injured black citizens.

*This building houses the Supreme Court in Washington, D.C.*

# SIX

# The Supreme Court Today

Today, the Supreme Court is equal to the legislative and executive branches of the federal government, politically and constitutionally. Although these other branches are larger, the Supreme Court is more powerful in some ways: it can declare laws passed by Congress unconstitutional and can declare the president's actions illegal. However, the Supreme Court can't abuse its power, because the other branches of government have ways of keeping it in check—by passing an amendment to the Constitution, for example.

In its relationship with the states, the Supreme Court has original jurisdiction in disputes between the federal and state governments, in suits between state governments, and in certain cases brought before it by a state. Under its appellate jurisdiction, the Supreme Court can review—and overturn—the decisions of the state supreme courts and can hear state cases in questions of federal law.

Yet the Supreme Court is just one part of the United States'

*In a lower court, a jury may hear a case.*

court system, which consists of state courts and federal courts. Each state has a court system and its own supreme court. If the state supreme court makes a decision based on a federal law or the Constitution, then the losing party may try to appeal that decision to the United States Supreme Court. (If the state court bases its decision only on state law, then the losing party can't appeal to the United States Supreme Court.)

The federal court system consists of the Supreme Court and the lower courts (96 district courts, 13 courts of appeal, and a number of special courts). The district courts, or federal trial courts, have original jurisdiction over federal civil and criminal cases, as well as suits between citizens of different states. The courts of appeal handle appeals from district courts and work as intermediates between the district courts and the Supreme Court. The special courts include the Tax Court, the Court of International Trade, the Court of Military Appeals, the Trademark Trial and Appeal Board, and the Claims Court. Appeals from the Tax Court go to a court of appeals; appeals from some of the special courts may go to another court, called the Court of Appeals for the Federal Circuit. Usually, all cases that start in the lower federal courts can be appealed ultimately to the United States Supreme Court. Thus the Supreme Court is the highest appeal court for all federal court cases and the final appeal court for state court cases that involve a question of federal law.

The United States Supreme Court consists of nine judges, or justices. Originally, when Congress set up the Supreme Court in 1789, it had only six justices. However, Congress increased the number of justices several times, and in 1869 the number was fixed at nine. The head justice is called the chief justice of the United States. The other justices are called associate justices.

To achieve the position of Supreme Court justice, a qualified candidate must be nominated by the president and confirmed by a majority vote of the Senate in a procedure similar to other important government appointments. Unlike elected government officials who serve for a set term (four years for the president, six years for a senator), justices serve a lifetime term (or until they resign). Some justices have served on the Court for more than 30 years. Justice William O. Douglas served the longest term—36 years—from 1939 until 1975. As a recess appointee (a person appointed—but not confirmed—during a Supreme Court recess), John Rutledge served the shortest term. He acted as chief justice for only one month in 1795 before the Senate rejected his appointment.

The only way to remove a Supreme Court justice from his office against his will is by impeachment, the same way that a president or a cabinet member is removed. To impeach a justice, the House of Representatives must vote charges against him, and then the Senate must try the charges and decide by a two-thirds vote to convict him and remove him from office. Only once in our history did the House vote to impeach a Supreme Court justice. This occurred in 1804, when the House charged Justice Samuel Chase of Maryland with using his judicial position to make political speeches against President Thomas Jefferson. However, the Senate failed to convict Chase by a two-thirds vote and he remained in office.

In 1982, the first woman justice joined the Supreme Court. Justice Sandra Day O'Connor was the 102nd justice appointed in the Supreme Court's history.

Today, the Supreme Court presides in Washington, D.C. Its building is near the Capitol where Congress convenes. Often referred to as the "marble palace," the impressive Supreme Court building houses the courtroom, the conference room, the justices' chambers, and the offices of the rest of the staff. However, the Supreme Court didn't always have such an impressive building. For many years, it did its work in makeshift offices in less-than-prestigious surroundings.

*Notable Supreme Court justices include Sandra Day O'Connor, the first woman justice, and William Hubbs Rehnquist, the sixteenth Chief Justice of the Supreme Court.*

*The Supreme Court building houses several libraries.*

A staff of about 320 people supports the justices. Most of these people—maintenance workers, security officers, and others who serve custodial and police functions—report to the marshal of the Court. About 30 employees do clerical work. The Court also has a reporter of decisions, who is in charge of preparing official records of Court decisions, and a librarian, who takes care of the libraries in the building. In addition, each justice has his own secretaries and law clerks.

The annual budget for the Supreme Court is very small compared to the budgets for the legislative and executive branches of the government. As is the case with most federal institutions, the money to run the Supreme Court comes from taxes. The chief justice is ultimately responsible for the management, maintenance, operation, and personnel of the Supreme Court.

*To hear both sides of a case, the Supreme Court allows one hour of Court time. Unless the lawyers receive an exception, they each have only 30 minutes to present their argument.*

# SEVEN

# How the Supreme Court Works

A large part of the Supreme Court's function is the same as that of any court, namely, to settle disputes between individuals. Many of these disputes are civil cases, which involve a suit by one person against another person, company, or the government seeking compensation for damages. For example, the Supreme Court heard a case in 1985 involving one soldier who killed another soldier while they were on leave. The victim's mother sued the United States government, claiming that the army should have known that the soldier who killed her son was dangerous because he previously had been convicted of killing someone else, and that it had been the army's responsibility to control and restrain him. The Supreme Court had to decide whether the army was required to pay damages to the victim's mother. The Court decided that the government was not responsible for the soldier's actions.

Other disputes involve criminal cases—those that are brought to punish someone for committing a crime. In 1985, the

*In a lower court, a jury often decides cases. The losing party may appeal the case to a higher court.*

Supreme Court heard a criminal case that involved Fourth Amendment rights, which protect against unreasonable searches of homes. In this case, police had searched a mobile home without a search warrant and had arrested someone based on their findings. According to the Fourth Amendment, a search warrant is required before a home may be searched. So the Court had to decide whether a mobile home was really a home. If the Court decided a mobile home could not be searched without a warrant, the police would have violated the defendant's Fourth Amendment rights. If the Court decided a mobile home was not protected under the Fourth Amendment, the police would not have violated his rights because a search warrant would not have been required. (The Court decided that the mobile home was not really a home—a decision that sent the defendant to prison.)

In both civil and criminal cases, the Supreme Court acts as an appellate, or appeals, court. Before a case can reach the Supreme Court for an appeal, a trial court must first hear the case. In the trial court, a jury or trial judge makes the original decision after hearing witnesses. After the trial, if the losing party feels that a mistake was made at the trial or that the decision against him was incorrect, he may appeal to a higher court. The appellate court doesn't hear witnesses' testimony again. Instead, it reads a brief (a written summary of the losing party's claims and other information), usually prepared by a lawyer, and listens to the lawyer make an oral presentation called an argument. Then the appeals court decides whether the trial court's decision was correct or not.

Each year, the state and federal courts decide hundreds of thousands of cases. About 4,000 of these cases are appealed to the Supreme Court. If the Supreme Court had to accept all of them, the justices would have to hear and write decisions on about 30 cases every working day—an impossible task. So the Supreme Court doesn't hear every case that is presented: the justices choose only the most important cases for appeal— usually about 200 cases each year. What makes a case important is the legal principle on which the lower court based its decision. If the principle causes problems for many lower courts, the Supreme Court will take the case so that its decision can give the courts guidance on the meaning of the law.

Besides appeals, the Supreme Court hears a small number of new cases each year that are within the Court's original jurisdiction. The only cases that fall into this category are ones involving disputes between the states, as when neighboring states fight over their border or when a state declares that its boundary extends farther than usual into international waters. Because of the importance of these disputes and the states' need for quick decisions, the Constitution provides original jurisdiction for them in the Supreme Court.

# The First Monday in October

For both civil and criminal cases, the Supreme Court hears arguments during its regular session, called the October term. It begins on the first Monday in October and usually ends in June or July of the following year. (The term's end date isn't set by any statutes or court rules.) At the end of the regular term, the chief justice announces a court order that states: "All cases submitted and all business before the Court at this term in readiness for disposition having been disposed of, it is ordered by this Court that all cases on the docket be, and they are hereby, continued to the next term."

After the regular term, the Supreme Court may hold a special session whenever necessary. The Court will hold a special session only when urgent matters arise that can't wait until the next regular term. For instance, the Court had to hold a special session to hear the *United States v. Nixon* case. In that case, it unanimously decided to order President Richard Nixon to release Watergate-related documents.

Before the Court opens for its regular term, the justices hold a conference to try to resolve matters leftover from the previous term. Then, on opening day, the Court can announce its rulings on these matters rather than delaying these rulings until later in the term.

For the rest of the regular term, the Supreme Court usually hears arguments on Monday, Tuesday, Wednesday, and occasionally Thursday for about seven two-week sessions. Between each two-week session, the justices take at least a two-week recess to think about the cases and to handle other Court business. Usually, the Court schedules four arguments a day from 10 A.M. to noon and from 1 P.M. to 3 P.M. Each argument is allowed 1 hour of Court time—30 minutes for each side. If a person thinks his case will take longer, he must get an exception to this time limit before the argument begins.

During the regular session, the Court also holds conferences every Friday—and sometimes on Wednesdays—to discuss the cases that the justices heard earlier in the week. They also review petitions and requests for future cases. Before each Friday conference, the chief justice prepares a "discuss list" that indicates the important cases requesting judicial review. Many cases on the list are never heard in Court because the justices decide that they're not important enough. Although the justices stop hearing arguments in April or May, they hold conferences until the session's end to discuss the remaining cases.

## How the Court Hears a Case

When the Court accepts a case for review, the court clerk must schedule a hearing. Usually a case must wait three month or more from the time it's scheduled until it is heard. A few weeks before the case is scheduled to be heard, the lawyer provides the justices with case records and a brief, which they are supposed to review before they hear the argument.

When it's time to hear the case, the Court prefers to hear only one lawyer speak per side, no matter how many lawyers

*Nixon waits in his office during the Watergate hearings.*

helped prepare the case. The Court expects the case's oral argument to highlight and clarify the information that appears in the brief. When a lawyer prepares for the oral argument, he must allow time for any questions that the justices want to ask him. For an average case, questions and remarks from justices take about one-third of the time allowed for the oral argument. Because the Court disapproves of arguments read from prepared texts, most lawyers work from notes or an outline so they remember to cover the most important points.

The Supreme Court tape-records and transcribes every oral argument it hears. During the session when the oral arguments are presented, only the justices and their law clerks can use the tapes. When they're not using them, the marshal of the court keeps them. At the end of the session, he turns them over to the national archives.

After they hear arguments for several cases, the Supreme Court justices discuss and decide them in conference. All conferences are held in complete secrecy in the conference chamber near the chief justice's office. No one other than the nine justices is permitted in the chamber during a conference. When the justices enter the room, they shake hands. To start the conference, the chief justice calls the first case to be decided. By tradition, each justice speaks in order: the chief justice starts the discussion, followed by the justice who has served on the Court the longest, then the next longest-serving justice, and so on until the justice with the least seniority speaks. We know very little about what actually happens during a conference. However, we do know that the Court rules allow each justice to speak for as long as he or she wants without interruption.

After the discussion, the justices vote on who should win the case. For voting, the order reverses: each justice votes in turn beginning with the most junior justice and ending with the chief justice. To decide a case, the Court must have a majority vote (five votes if all nine of the justices are involved).

**Justices discuss cases in the conference chamber.**

The justices don't announce the vote immediately. First, they write an opinion—a document that announces the decision and the reasoning behind it. Writing the opinion can take less than a week or more than six months, depending on the complexity of the case. The most senior justice who voted with the majority selects the justice to write the majority opinion. Any other justices may write a separate opinion—a concurring opinion if they agree with the majority opinion but not with the reasons behind it, or a dissenting opinion if they disagree with the majority opinion. Other justices may sign a concurring or dissenting opinion.

When a justice is assigned to write the majority opinion, law clerks may sort through the information needed to write the draft. When the draft is ready, the information office prints a limited number of copies so it can circulate to the other justices for their comments. Sometimes justices may change their votes

77

when they see the draft majority opinion and the dissenting opinion. If enough justices change their votes, the original decision may be reversed. Then the opinion-writing process starts again.

When the opinions have been written and reviewed, the Supreme Court announces its majority opinion and its dissenting opinion or opinions. This is the first time that the Court's decision is made public. The opinions are not only announced in Court, but copies are also given to courtroom lawyers and reporters as well as to the Court's public information office. Then the reporter of decisions sees that the opinions are published in the *United States Reports*, and the public information officer releases the opinions to the news media.

## Time-Honored Traditions

Although the Supreme Court is trying to pare down its procedures and to cope more efficiently with change, it is still the

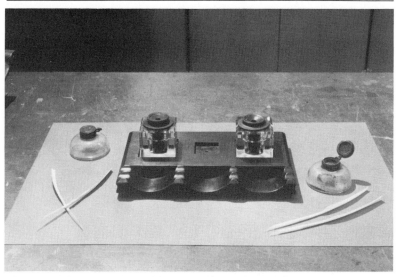

*Using quill pens is an old Supreme Court tradition.*

*Justices shake hands to symbolize their unity of purpose.*

most traditional branch of the government. Strict observance of historical traditions has helped maintain its image of dignity, caution, and substance—a fitting one for the nation's highest court. Such an image also matches the public's idea of Supreme Court justices—individuals of integrity who are wise, full of high purpose, and untouched by external influences.

Some Supreme Court traditions are curiously old-fashioned, such as the use of quill pens made from goose feathers, and the full-time employment of a seamstress to mend the justices' robes. Other Supreme Court traditions are more practical.

Secrecy is one of the oldest Court traditions. This tradition is important because disclosure of conference proceedings could lower the public's regard for the Court and its decisions. Similarly, justices refrain from talking to others about conflicts among themselves because they don't want to lessen the Court's dignity or encourage more conflict.

Whether they're in or out of Court, the Supreme Court justices try to maintain an aura of courtesy and formality—another long-standing tradition. Whenever the justices enter the courtroom or begin a private conference, they shake hands to symbolize their harmony of purpose, which should be stronger than any differences of opinion they may have. When the justices express themselves in Court or in written opinions, they

*The curved bench lets all of the justices see the courtroom.*

address the others as "my brothers" or even "my dissenting brothers." Justices tend to maintain respectful personal relations with each other: they rarely voice disagreement or irritation. When they do, they may criticize a justice subtly by pointing out how his previous speeches or opinions disagree with his current opinion.

The seniority system is yet another established tradition that affects most of the Court's work. The justices discuss cases in order of seniority and vote on cases in order of reverse seniority. The most junior justice is always assigned the task of gathering the documents and other information needed by the Court. Even the justices' courtroom seating is based on seniority. They all sit at a winged mahogany bench, with the chief justice at the center. To his right sits the senior associate justice, and to his left sits the associate justice with the next highest seniority. The rest of the justices sit at the bench in an alternating pattern of seniority with the most junior justice seated at the far left and the second most junior justice seated at the far right. Seniority even determines assignment of office space. The Court building has a set of bronze doors that seal off seven suites of offices from the public, so the two junior justices must occupy the offices just outside of these doors.

The Supreme Court's traditional image of stability and continuity reflects its nature. One reason for the Court's stable image is that justices are appointed for life, so the same justices serve for many years. Vacancies rarely occur, so turnover is low. The Court's reliance on legal precedents in deciding cases also adds to its image of continuity.

Not everyone agrees with all of the Supreme Court traditions. Some practices are controversial, such as lifetime service. Some opponents support mandatory retirement for justices when they reach a specified age. Another Supreme Court tradition that has come under fire is its secrecy. Opponents are seeking televised Court sessions. But for now, the Supreme Court continues to rely on its time-honored traditions.

*Bronze doors seal off seven justices' offices. Two junior justices have offices on the public corridor outside.*

# EIGHT

# A Final Look

The Supreme Court holds a key position in the United States government that often surprises foreign visitors. They wonder why it should hold a position equal to the Congress and the president, who are elected by millions of citizens. Whereas the president controls the army and navy and heads an executive department with millions of people working for him, the nine Supreme Court justices aren't elected, but appointed, and they have only a small support staff working for them.

The Supreme Court has this equal position because of its important function: interpreting the Constitution for all citizens. This function often involves defining the extent of the power of other government branches. During the Watergate affair, when President Nixon resisted handing over some presidential tapes, the Supreme Court had the power to make him do so. When members of Congress passed a law limiting the amount of money that people could contribute to election campaigns, the Supreme Court ruled against the Congress, calling such restrictions unconstitutional.

Supreme Court ruled against the Congress, calling such restrictions unconstitutional.

The Court's responsibility for interpreting the Constitution also has an impact on state governments, because the Court can overturn laws passed by state legislatures and decisions made by state supreme courts on issues of federal law.

Perhaps the Supreme Court's most important role is that of guardian of our basic freedoms. Although the Bill of Rights guarantees these freedoms, the Court must protect them from government encroachment and the tyranny of the majority, who could pressure Congress to pass laws that might violate the freedoms of the minority.

Because of the wide-ranging impact of the United States Supreme Court, much political discussion and activity has focused on it. Organizations that oppose the Supreme Court's rulings on the issues of school prayer and abortion have begun large-scale campaigns to get those decisions overturned. News-

*The Supreme Court ruled against school prayer in 1962. Some organizations still lobby to overturn this decision.*

papers have devoted a great deal of space to the Court's rulings on such things as videotape pirating and vetoes of administrative rules by Congress. During the 1984 presidential election, people speculated about the types of Supreme Court justices each candidate might appoint and how the new appointees might affect the Court's direction.

Yet these reactions should come as no surprise. Throughout our history, the Court has been a subject of great interest in political arenas. After all, it plays a critical role in resolving many of the country's important and controversial issues. And in doing so, the Supreme Court shapes the government's policies in such diverse areas as environmental protection and civil rights.

Although people may think of the Supreme Court as nonpolitical, this label is inaccurate. The Court is a vital part of the government, so by definition, it's political. Most of the justices have a political background, and their appointments to the Court are frequently subject to politics. The Court's political nature surfaces when it rules on cases brought by special interest groups and when its decisions are affected by the justices' views of public and congressional opinion. The decisions themselves can lead to heated political debates in the government and throughout the nation. Congressional representatives and other political figures may even attack the justices if they disagree with their decisions.

Some people feel that the Supreme Court has become too active in politics, that its major decisions and legal interpretations have had too much influence on public policies. They often point to the Court's rulings on abortion, segregation, and capital punishment as examples of national policy-making by judicial decision. They believe that the Supreme Court should restrain itself in such matters.

But many disagree. By its very nature, the Supreme Court is limited as a policymaker and has little or no chance to abuse

*Court-ordered desegregation led to forced busing.*

its power. Its limitations take three major forms. First, it can only hear a relatively small number of cases each year. Compared with other policy-making agencies, it deals with a very limited number of policy issues. Second, even the most active justices believe in judicial restraint in certain cases. Sometimes the Court will refuse to hear cases that might be devastatingly controversial, such as legal disputes over America's involvement in the Vietnam war. Third, other policymakers can limit the effect of the Court's decisions. For instance, if the Court inter-

*Antibusing groups pressured Congress to change busing laws.*

prets tax laws in a way that causes problems, the Congress can change the tax laws. If the Court orders school desegregation, the lower courts and school boards can form their own policies for implementation.

As a part of the federal government, the United States Supreme Court is not all-powerful, but it is an essential and unique institution. As long as conflicts and controversies exist, we will need a court system to settle them. And as long as the United States has a Constitution, we will need the Supreme Court to interpret it and to protect the rights that it grants.

87

# GLOSSARY

Appeal—To take a case to a higher court for review.

Argument—Oral presentation of a case made by a lawyer.

Brief—A short, written summary of the claims and pertinent information relating to a case.

Case—A court action to protect rights or redress wrongs.

Decision—The judgment made by a court when settling a case.

Diversity case—A case involving citizens of different states.

Due process—Fair and usual procedures, such as the right to a fair trial and the right to face one's accusers.

Incriminate—To charge with or show evidence of involvement in a crime.

Judgment—A court's official decision based on a full review of the case.

Jurisdiction—The power to interpret or apply the law.

Mandamus—A court order that directs a lower court or other authority to perform a specific act.

Opinion—A written explanation of the legal principles on which a Supreme Court decision is based.

Overrule—To overturn or reverse a previous decision.

Writ—A written court order commanding the person who receives it to perform or not perform acts that it specifies.

# SELECTED REFERENCES

Baum, Lawrence. *The Supreme Court*. 2d ed. Washington, D.C.: Congressional Quarterly, Inc., 1984.

Congressional Quarterly, Inc. *Guide to the U. S. Supreme Court*. Washington, D.C.: Congressional Quarterly, Inc., 1979.

Friedman, Leon, and Israel, Fred L., eds. *The Justices of the United States Supreme Court, 1789-1978*. 5 vols. New York: Chelsea House Publishers, 1980.

Halpern, Stephen C., and Lamb, Charles M. *Supreme Court Activism and Restraint*. Lexington, Mass.: Lexington Books, 1982.

Hamilton, Alexander, et al. *The Federalist Papers*. Edited by Clinton Rossiter. New York: New American Library (Mentor Books), 1961.

Harrell, Mary Ann. *Equal Justice Under Law: The Supreme Court in American Life*. Washington, D.C.: The Foundation of the Federal Bar Association with the National Geographic Society, 1975.

Jackson, Robert H. *The Supreme Court in the American System of Government*. Cambridge: Harvard University Press, 1955.

Ulmer, S. Sydney, ed. *Courts, Law, and Judicial Processes*. New York: Free Press, 1981.

---

**ACKNOWLEDGMENTS**

The author and publishers are grateful to these organizations for information and photographs: Joan Andrew; AP/Wide World Photos; Collection of the Supreme Court of the United States; Delaware River Port Authority; Eastern National Park and Monument Association; Jack Kightlinger, The White House; Library of Congress; Lincoln University, Oxford, Pa.; Maryland Historical Society, Baltimore; Roxie Munroe; National Archives; National Portrait Gallery, Smithsonian Institution; The New York Times Company; Superior Court of the District of Columbia; Supreme Court Historical Society; U. S. House of Representatives; UPI/Bettmann Newsphotos; Washington Post, reprinted by permission of the D.C. Public Library; Betty Wells, NBC. Photo research: Imagefinders, Inc. Cartoon research: Richard Samuel West of *Target, The Political Cartoon Quarterly*.

# INDEX

reckless disregard 57
Rehnquist, William Hubbs 68
religion, establishment of 58
reporter of decisions 69
retirement 51, 81
*Roe v. Wade* 61
Roosevelt, Franklin D. 49-51
Rutledge, John 21, 67

## S

*Schenck v. United States* 54, 55
schools 17, 57-58, 84, 87
Scott, Dred 36, 42
Scottsboro boys 60
search warrant 58, 59, 72
secrecy 76, 79, 81
segregation 17, 62-63, 85-87
Senate 19, 21, 67-68
seniority 76, 80-81
separate but equal 52, 62-63
separation of powers 8, 27
Sherman Antitrust Act 46
Sixteenth Amendment 32, 46
Sixth Amendment 60
slavery 13, 36, 42, 43, 45
Soviet Union 54
special session 74
Story, Joseph 34
supremacy clause 35

## T

Taney, Roger B. 40, 41
tax 38, 46, 69, 86
Tax Court 66-67
term, Court 74
Trademark Trial and Appeal
    Board 67
treaties 19, 20, 34
trial by jury 25
Twenty-sixth Amendment 32
tyranny of the majority 27, 84

## U

unions 48
*United States Reports* 78
United States Treasury 38
*United States v. Nixon* 74

## V

Vietnam 15, 56
voting, justices' 76-77, 80

## W

Washington, George 8, 16, 21
*The Washington Post* 56
Watergate 14, 74, 75, 83
*Weeks v. United States* 58
*West Virginia Board of Education
    v. Barnette* 57
World War I 53
World War II 11